Circus by Moonlight

Mark Van Aken Williams

LUCKY PRESS, LLC
ATHENS, OHIO

Published by:
Lucky Press, LLC
PO Box 754
Athens, OH 45701-0754

Email: books@luckypress.com
Phone: 614-309-0048
Website: www.luckypress.com
SAN: 850-9697

ISBN-13: 978-0-9760576-6-6
ISBN-10: 0-9760576-6-2

Library of Congress Control Number: 2009903875

Printed in the United States of America

For additional copies, call 866-308-6235 (ext. 6) and ask for
Circus by Moonlight by ISBN: 0-9760576-6-2.
Lucky Press books are also available on Amazon.com and
through special order at your local bookstore. Visit
www.luckypress.com for our latest titles.

Table of Contents

Circus by Moonlight

flanked by a quiet of night
they watch
the parade, migrating
circus figures,
passing in unfamiliar
outlines of pygmy
rotundity
and ballooning-bubble-elasticity.

limp sleepers, hanging
by moon's hooking crescent,
space babies with
no planet, dangling
to the organ grinder's
hypnotic spell,
while cotton candy —
cocoon, envelopes them, in sticky.

What the Hell Am I Doing?

to start is always
just letting the mind
limber up

you're not quite sure
when the hidden resources
between synapses

and that mysterious region
that creates the things
we know not where they

had an origin or impression
will awaken
and extricate itself

if in fact it is a self
living and feeding like
a leech on our dreams

every now and then regurgitating
a picture
a smell

that prods us like cattle
to at least try to
put it down

or put a smile on our face
perhaps a story or
welsh-like sentence

the kind you need to
read over and over again
just marveling

marveling

Solitary Signs

i come from this wall,
but not as graffiti,
with cryptic lettering
that declares the
boundaries of suffrage,
extracted from a child's
innocence — blood still warm.

i am not a thick
moss, the mold of suffocation come to
seal forever an offensive mortar, a tomb for our
sins under a lush
and deceptive green.

i am born of a seed,
deposited unseen by a
breath that was gentle
as a lover's sigh, to
draw support through
the decay, a blooming,
simple and susceptible.

Grab It When You Can

had a chance
when the circus came to town
to scratch
the need
turning round and round

had a chance
to carve initials in a tree
when the pocketknife
was sharp
and sufficient

had a chance
to ask for a dance
while the girls
were fanning their innocence
across an empty floor

had a chance
when the moment was perfect
and nothing could miss
for a boy
competing at mumbletypeg

The Dialogue

try not to burden
me with things
that i have never felt
under the influence
of weightlessness

tell me again about
feather-weighted bones
that will carry me
beyond the lamp which
lights the lifting

speak carefully when
addressing the environment
of uncertainty
for solar flares will
assault the principle

i tend to enjoy the
part where pine boughs
fall upon the headstone
far below the floating
moon where wildly i spin

Not Here, You Don't

there's nothing going down here.
no long cool players speaking
in cut-off phrases, that tell
stories in themselves — hip riffs.

no music from alley basements,
sounding the call of night games,
the hand come on — crotch grabbing
to telegraph an intention.

there's nothing going down here.
no stretch limos thumping low
rider samples, with fog cutters
leading the way — ships over america.

no airwaves leading the religious.
sounding the call of barefoot
babies, crawling towards a dew
covered dawn — fields of redemption.

When Comes the Guitar Electric

what is it about
hard edged guitar
     cutting
     clean grooves
air-streamed sounds
that excite
     something in our
     scale
kind of religious

i feel lighter

is it some tribal
instinct
     bang those bones
     string the bow
to fire arrows
at the sun
     curving in an
     arch — to fall again
listening for the
scream

i am invisible

is it a heart
     meter
jacked up higher
like a balloon
     so near the saber's
     blade — a silver flash
pounding
     against
     rib cage
involuntary ticking

i am closer to the heart
     — wah wah

A Sweater Day

today has the first
chill of the year.
a sweater day —
one to once again
unseal the drawer,
slightly fastened
and dormant, the
one with six layers of jaundice-flesh
paint, the legacy
of previous tenants.

it will take this
day to discharge
the sour measure of
mothball-musk, an
asphyxiating balm
with its momentary
etherreality — a foggy
climate. where
the last hope for
indian summer dulls
under anesthesia.

The Writer as a Child

this is an open letter
to children who
verily cannot put feelings

into their own correspondence
because i could never get past
that defective first recognition

but do not ache
because it was the convention
that censored the attempt

so don't rely on formality
but hold to your heart all impressions
and disclose them later

when the competence matches
our automatic assimilation
of powerful perceptions

it's there
waiting for the right time
as your substance synthesizes

Summer Evening Chorus

popsicle traces on the horizon
sweeping like sparklers across
july fourth nostalgia-skies
children with red and green
smiling sticky mouths
racing liquid down to the wood

laughing at each other with
different-colored tongues

Rocking Chair

the ivy
has outstretched
its
welcome,

prowling with
implication
over porch
towards
my rocker.

it has
been
too long
since
last your

gentle cadence
has
soothed
this aging
backbone,

too long
forgotten
the utility
of
your rhythm.

The Idea of Falling

smelt the canicular days
from my liver
the severity from my stomach
the public perturbations

aerodynamics in the ascendant
be they coagulated
livid or lumpish are
not to discomfort or be divided

Our Remedial Estate

in a supermarket aisle
you can notice a care-worn person
suck dry his mannerism.
set about his behavior:
(diverted thoughts)
practicing and working
upon itself.

altering some course in life;
observe by his countenance,
gestures and momentum, what it is that
offends him.

the manner of it,
can awaken an unexpected alteration
of your own monstrous
and ineffable minutia:
our tragic stories

The Truth about Anger

the queen of the senses
is not our divine music,
the presbytery tonality that
pacifies our wraithy soul;
dancing air into the body.

it is the hectic flush of asperity
which is the sovereign
remedy against despair,
in its liberal science and
mercenary consideration.

there is no heart without it.
players or jesters who can
ease us in an instant know this;
their wit and ministry, the
magnifier of requisite marrow.

In Apogee

under the moon
appeared an errant planet
slightly corrupted.

with discontent and envy
it failed to appropriate
god's grace.

an inkling in false motives,
the juggled patterns of light,
exhumed the secret of its sin.

slowly, the wax of
feminine caesura revealed an
independent strategy

of self protection and
self management:
by the sleight of the moth.

Basement of Birth

a birth can come from
body, mind, or fortune.

the deformities can be
unlearned or circumstantial.

seldom, said Plutarch, do
honesty and beauty abide in each other.

Hannibal had only one eye, but the
retina of the soul perceives the best—

anyway. and Socrates was as
hairy as an ape.

Fortunae Telum, Non Culpae

fortune's fault will not be mine,
if you become abstracted by it,

for i am the scullion in the eye
of infinite ethnicities,

surpassing all that subtlety can give —
the fatigue which will be housed in

marble and gold, makes us
equal for a second. this is when

the capital of nature becomes
contemptable and blameworthy.

A Cakewalk into Town

what i didn't want to say

is just that
i can't look back anymore

because i need another way
i estimate
to learn what is good

and what i am to be

i can listen to old records
to hear about what is between
me

and that world outside

but it is not real
only alienating
myself into the inane

and time is so short
to be incomplete

loneliness now beyond probabilities

so here i go into the unknown

[wow – this shit is scary]

but what the hell
other people do it also
at least in those old records
when a certain dude sings
about that cakewalk into
town

[and baby don't you want to go?]

you bet!

i wouldn't mind a roll in my pocket
a nice shirt perfumed
a little but not too much

with that small chance
that someone who is pretty
not exquisite
only fair
could find me pleasing

and we could swing on a steady roll

doo doo dee
and a
doo doo dee

The Mad Round of Sainthood

it will be safer, more desirable, and historical
than penance—even embarrassment itself will
adopt and live on little with content.

so when virtue visits from the canopy's treasury,
i will desire no more than ideas and anima,
to be engraved on my obscurity.

The Circumscription

i am a finer
subjugator
than the devil.
he has his goods
and good name,
but where are
his descendants,
let alone
his smugness, and
cronies in chorus.

when he loses
his sinews,
all confidence
will be half-awake,
for fools know
nothing of facility,
or *coelum cogitaveris;*
if you would but
meditate on me.

he forgets about
this one who will
endure what rage
and fury can invent,
the ganglion of
sweet reason
to embrace.

Miserably Happy or Happily Miserable

Everyone is the orchardist of his own odds.
The mind is more effectual than election.

No one is embittered except by himself.
Leading him to the bevel of suffrage.

Men in themselves will forget fatherhood.
As birds are crapulous with henbane.

Will worsen into a discourse of instinct.
Exceptional in expense, they come to be sadists.

The pyretic circle is only a bias.
One needs a control, the other a condolence.

What an infelicity of misadventure, this.
One deceives, the other instructs.

Ganymede in Heaven

the rain is a macula to dry land,
as braided stream is to the
intransparency of Neptune's bowels.

the genius is an alien to anatomy,
yet so rewarding in whimsicality
and coign of vantage.

all such conceits are incurious
of our fretted roof, and in the
especial care of parochialists.

to find more sublimity with
god and retinue, this variety
of scheme will make our amends.

Landscape

no sign of thunder
or any
illustration

only miles
and many miles
around
         . . . swimming

more than any weather
can say

or beauty
because it is truly
beautiful

a sea of seas
a trace
of sweet grass . . .

simply

Remnant of Dinner

the empty plate was
left in the kitchen,

a crusty fossil
in the lonely cold

and voiceless hours
of mice and phantasm.

Where You Lie, While You Lie

plenty of stars
have passed you by
lying there dreaming
about faces and scenes
that are not part
of your day

settling down with
bags and belongings
in the rafters
to pull
at your eyelids
with their smiles
and lullabies

adopting an essential
occasion to trace
the distinction
while a song repeats
about how
one morning
you will be mine

In the Zone

i know it seems funny
but it keeps getting harder to
see that this can
be an address

   though

i want to live like this
in a world
stuck within the
ripe moments

   before

the curious
and the lunatics
said that there was
a vacancy for us

   by

stroke of luck
it will come back as
a personal
asylum

We Are the First Story

is it foolish
to get our necks
so entangled,
wrapped serpent-like,
writhing in a pit,
where the blackness
seems to move.
for the temptation
is only
a story told before
our inclination
had any ambition.
and it doesn't
feel like we have
any misery
here,
coiled in our fall.

The Rehearsal

i am rehearsing for
the rehearsal,
running over the lines,
and trying to figure out
how to get it right.
wondering where i will be
when the curtain calls.

there is no attire.
no cloak or character.
for correctness
is improvisation
and there is no validity
in judgment.
no solace in conjecture.

If You Make It My Problem

i do not believe that i
have ever encountered
someone as sullen as
the man downstairs

[keep it to yourself . . . man!]

there is contempt in his intercourse
that makes guilt come
like it is everybody else's
crime

what is in that receding-hairlike
shell of consternation?

just once, i would like to
slap him silly

and see how i feel

. . . about it

Just Thinking

i wonder if i
speak the language anymore
or ever did

though words come
tripping
out on their own

usually in response
to the outer limits
of others

or as
inscrutable
airing

pretending
to be
thought

or perhaps
just
waiting . . .

Spotting Marigolds

marigolds of the ages were
shadows, past the corners
and living ahead.
spending moments, strained,
to grasp a look. to focus.

yellow memories across
lost generations take me
all the way. knowing
the way she moves, teaches
me that i'm alive.

the red and yellow steal
my heart away. glimpsing
around the corners and
dancing through the bind,
blossoms become the truth.

What Is It in Them Books?

story, oh the story
is that which i love so much.
that which brings me back to
the books
that my dogs crave for their
glue addiction, trying
to comport an innocence, even though
the stain of dye upon their
beards, unknown to them,
reveals the beautiful deep red
of binding.
and oddly offense eludes me
for my thoughts only hope
that the carcass was as satisfying
for them as
the marrow was for me.

Winter's Hour

was it the arthritis which pained
bare knees? climbing the planked
stairs, through a black void
committed to memory, a spider web
against the day's beard. step by
painful step, sharper and sharper
the hurt came to call and take
residence in the parlor, like an
unwelcomed guest. another sheet
for the furniture. or was it just
the night cold prodding the joints
up to a bird-feathered warmth, to
nurture the wee hours of his ascent?

Wind in the Labyrinth

endless was the image,
seemingly high above,
high as the hiss of
a scorched wind (and low as the
    estimate of it),

a labyrinth to its garden
lesson
or a monk who tills the
hours amoung our
texts,
never knowing the pangs
of love (to moisten the ink with
    tears),
or the poverty of loss.

just endless and unforgivable.

Fantasy

how caprice
is
a
dance on windowpane

consider
the
buoyancy and balance

on one leg
then another
over and over again
till

the traffic
is not
so whirl-wind-ish

just happy

Ash and Bone

little known of what
these bones
have versed, the

weight and transpiring
marrow these eyes
may receive; not so

different to a larger
brain. it is our link,
to have shared

so many things, estranged
only by a linear
scale, which prescribes

my privilege, my understanding.
but without question
or pride, do i

begin to imagine
that the vision is any
fairer from this tenure.

Carrying Spears

the tiny
scurrying
bug

had a bit
part
indeed

on such a
dramatic
leaf

halfway to
epic
extent

In a Crowd

hungry
and deceived by the crush of
emotion,
slithering snake-like
through the
huddled parcels of sacred
ground.
a novelty of
connection, or appearance
of mass, is the mystery
we make and
the link to our fears.

Sometimes, the Hostile. Always a Blooming.

in open and hostile territory,
a fugitive from interiors,
the marigolds open
reddened eyes — a blinding strain
from a secret world.
one where the bees are
no longer naive and coy,
but live to pursue — and
defend the mint to the death.

tottering over ant hills,
words are separate — polar
regions that repel each step,
carried off on backs with
military order. but a primary
desire to stay the impasse,
restores that window picture
which was once inviting — and
the world becomes a waiting bud.

Listening to "Kind of Blue"

the timbre of the blues
    — doped up
slower than i remember
    — a nod
making mellow on
all sides
without any
noise
coming through
walls
the yelling and
broken dishes
    — plasterboard
    thumps
the familiar contest
left to neighbors
while
a heavy weight
    — of saxophone
    and trumpet
intoxicates the
whole
    — context

Believe You Me

there is a place for us
devoid of homesickness
where there are things
not of this world
no mistakes of the unlucky
and the play is simple—
a reminder of childhood
a belief in ourselves—
oh to be ourselves

A Bit of History at My Feet

there is history in the fallen leaf,
short and prosaic and unwritten.

i stand looking down at a seasoned
casualty, in fastened animation.

had you forsaken the lure of sugar
or tired of the season's caress.

there are no coins on your eyes
and mourners' wails are wind bourn.

anonymous member of the chorus,
perhaps i had heard your voice sing

with the current, a rustling comfort
that piloted me to sleep and dreams.

did you provide a cool shade when
i had cursed the dog day heat,

connected by the umbilical of your
host to the mother of us all.

yes — you had a history, short and
unwritten, but to me it was poetry.

Somewhere, Sometime

i might be on the moon swimming
in one of those moon-dust seas,
or getting a cool blue shade tan
from the spinning top above.

i might be taking a noon-day nap,
stretched out and lazy in my
orchid chaise among the rainforest
canopy; watchman of all things small.

i might be riding the gulf current
bringing presents to your shores,
with coconuts full of america's
milk, consumated by native tears.

i might be a witness to your silent
crimes, innocent and undetected,
with mouth taped and bloody wrists
struggling to unleash the burning.

i might be a child's voice, unspoiled,
filling the apse with wafting angelic
self-possession, that reminds you of
an innocent scene within your nature.

i might be holding your hand as we
approach the river's edge, listening
to the water rippling over perfectly
smooth pebbles and the grasshoppers' songs.

The Selfish Trap

it was empty as a stare,
just short of the truth.
>*giving is inversely*
>*related.*

it was nervous as a laugh,
just short of satire.
>*giving is inversely*
>*related.*

it was a tall garden maze,
where false routes deceive.
>*giving is inversely*
>*related.*

it was counterfeit currency,
for comfort comes from the soul.
>*giving is inversely*
>*related.*

Game of Spinning Children

all the children sing
as the swirling world
of green and blue
blend, deflecting
any orientation in
their suspension of
reality; puppets
tangling the
long-umbilicals.

the brain is
swimming within its
soft furtherance,
and brings blood to
the border-world
where vision steals
the fire and brings
it back to a place
that knows no exploit.

raise your hands
skyward and feel the
passion spread you
outward to the
far-universe
until all of creation is within
and becomes
your domain.

Open-Water Encounter

why do dolphins always appear at our bow
to ride the compulsive current-waves,

turning an eye and a smile upward through
the jet stream clearness of thick pane,

not yet the trailing foam of our passing,
fusing our glance for an instance,

only to bail out like a rocket streamer
and fade into the blue depths of memory?

Planning the Course, Maybe

putting off everything.
something within me
that just can't
construct plans and
inflict the act
like those obsessive
calculators who never
live their lives
for reason of scheduling,
yet can't help but
magistrate mine.

                    but,
where is the danger
in following what
guides each destiny
through currents or tides?
the source which makes
each person distinct.

there is no prize
at the end, only what
the heart can entertain
as it siphons life
in a regular and
undeniable cadence,
true to its own
rhythm

perhaps i have a plan
to put off the jury.

Homily

preacher
said some words
said something

they were lines around
my eyes
i expect

Too Square to Boogie

too bad
that
music box
has
no rhythm

kind'a like
a ballerina rotating
on
one foot

Summer Chimes the Self

the sounds of
summer
are no more
trenchant than
approaching chimes
of the ice cream truck,
bringing to your
corner
an expectation
which tickles the
ingredients
of your first connection,
the genesis of
a theology.

China

Stand behind the tree so
paper tigers can't see you.

The reactionaries swing from
branches, dodging falling bricks.

We can all sleep safely while
the wind bells softly chime,

As the hexagon hardens and
the onion rots in the clay.

Between Seconds

having a moment that
was free
something unable
to be shared

the light of the sun
swirled me 'round
to it
raising the mercury

and i floated
while the clock
hands pointed toward
a lapse

so surreal
that words would
corrupt the empathy
somewhere between seconds

Could Be Doric, Could Be Analogous

the column that sponsors the weight
has its spell on all
between, neither lost nor found,
before a boundary is crossed
or a sacrifice can be made on sacred ground.

seems like plenty of room down on the floor,
from this distance, careful that
it doesn't crumble as the appearance
might suggest.

oh the age.

That Song I Liked So Much
But Could Never Figure Out Why

come to the lucky palace
where the chance to lose
is nothing but that
garcia lyric
because it's true i know now

a deal
only a deal

and isn't it really the way
things unfold anyway
nothing left to lose
so you
can't

Pillars Rising

carrying the brick
in hand.
dry,
red clay under nail,
moving from
place to place
to place.
i — if not a brick,
but the hand —
captivate,
survey,
looking to assemble
form and shape,
although certain boundaries
have clung to my skin
as paste.
and a coagulation
heals the wounds
between layers and layers
that rise as pillars
and encompass
the construction.

The Spotlight of Scrutiny

the tenor has beads of sweat,
slow moving, with developing
tributaries, like rivers on
a map — each branching out in
its distinct route toward an
ocean. salt eternally returns
home, just as salmon must depart.

the voice is capable to induce
a passion, yet the beads are
imploring a departure, singular
death leaps. lemming at the cliff.
and the descent is so graceful
as my eyes chase the glistening
droplets downward with profundity.

A Speck of Grit

what's that in the
corner of my eye?
a stepping ladder,
so i can see you.

what's that thing
out of dimension,
but not my sight?
something tattered.

are the tears for
washing clear,
imprinted apparitions?
canals of creation.

am i rubbing away
the affliction?
or grinding at grit,
with a finger once pointed.

Hygienic Humor

ooey, he said, isn't this the
        good life.
and i said, yes sir, the greatest
        show on earth.

yes we really had a good belly
        laugh.
good enough to hang it out with
        the laundry.

Revelation

in individual time
it takes only
a second
to claim sovereignty

sooner or later
there it is
the secret moment
revealed to
the part confused by
alternatives

speaking for itself

one's own
implicit differentiation

A Fisherman's Oblation

the flock of gulls breathes above;
an undulating mass that expands and
contracts, each thought of constituency
not quite sure whether to descend
or retreat, overpowered by, and drunk
with purpose, a seduction born from
a fisherman's offering, parts of
carcass ditched to the rocks below
his dangerous plank, cold and jagged
to less discerning eyes, where the
syncopated collision of waves against
them suggest collusion and context.

Secret Agent Man

this is a report
to verify
nothing

because all is nothing
but grapevine

anyway

Finger Walking Can Give You Calluses

in a certain light the words
of the prophets resemble
the yellow pages—

only yellower.

Sailfish

break the ceiling
and startle your way
towards the fireball sun;
spying for briefest
of moments
thing-monster
which has its grasp
so relentless —
giving way till
the potency returns.
shake it out.
spit it back,
that sharp snag,
with the sting of
Poseidon's trident.

Snickering

fat and huffing
lady,
wields a screaming
lawnmower,

swearing at nothings,
deaf
to the children's
snickering.

Composition of Compensation

anything that could be handcrafted
in animal charcoal
black and white andante tempo
does not drag its slow length along

that which goes by the denomination
of art is a belligerent
once meant to be the animating force,
the vital fluid, of the possible,
the Apostles' creed, and scullion of
innumerable biographies

the clockworks are demiurgic
a long farewell when you find
yourself embosomed by
anxious and mystified affiliations
to wave aside the devil and all

the composition will be even more
a rarity
than any pregnant excursionist
look among the human family
it is from among them that there
will burst forth a work of which will
be a just amend to all the animal
kingdom

The Drive-by Was the First Fly-by

the bar-coded bird of Minerva will suffer a hit and run
by other birds, because of its celebrated plumage

all the highlands through their altimetry will
be as naked as the jaybird in the lunar landscape

better that she be red-faced by fall of the year
when there is no one to fly to the assistance of

when every bladder has ten gallons of wine
the stormy petrel will be pie-eyed in the midst

so that the parable of the jars will volley them
at close quarters and clip their wings

Suit the Action to the Profession

in the vanishing parcels, the
jellyfish are labile to their fashion

in an ornamental border
terriers play an important part

for the hounding of bones
is a common practice in forensics

often those in bad odor are
to turn one's nose at

in the sure bet that their mere
lungs would have no vacation

some have dibs on ready wit and
mastermind the analgesic, while

the fishy ink slinging of the humorist
has made the manual a forgery

Funny Feeling

a few attenuate souls will shift the
cast of countenance

they will arrive in league and
piece together the loaves and fishes

in this womb of time there will be no
algorithm in the wild of sand

our calm was a false deathlike calm
a similar chicane to the shallow-draft

our pub-crawl was predicated under
the configuration of an animal

the feigning were given the
nod to manic seizures

but our stomachs will not sink
nor will any of us be in default

Religion, Violence, and Reconciliation

do not detonate
clause and catchword
because i also
can brandish
my quintic quiver

your quarrel is not
as politic as mine
because when
impressed on the
heart, i draft the living

The Particulars

we are lunatics for the curiosity
the wonders of the moment

already we are what they want
and they have become epidemic

Glottalic Airstream

lips move
but the modulation
is unconnected

a disjunct of
community meshing
similar spaces

Appointed Time

one's move will present itself
at the wholesale hour

some conclude that it is
loitering obliquely

not making any issue
of a smile at misadventure

there may seem to be
interim at the bursting point

this is the faceless
quiddity of our intimate

designed to draw out
chance and faith

so when i use the verb
"to awaken"

it does not merely mean
to come to oneself

because appointed time
does not occur in a void

Shakes, Shivers, and Dithers

brigandines, breastplates,
the thrill of fear is cinctured
as a wall of water,
the course, as Apis
pole vaulting
the dog-day cicada

in flood, at flood
rambling
madmen be word-bound
be a stimulus of undercurrent

the angle of vision
will have the last
guess-word
the hubris of vision
will be the last
airy tale of empty space

Comic Entertainment

the district of the kidneys is
assumed to be a repertory of
the culinary art

to prepare a pie for the afterpiece
is one of the most meandering
recipes faced by the style

the cluster of vesicles
is always on our lips
but far from the vital appendage

the audition of aspect is set
for the day of butchery
and the advent of company

The Wonderful Promise

news arrived of a friend who climbed Everest
which brought about a mensuration

and my mountain stood before me
from where i will not be brought back down

Seek Me and Live

i was looking for a repeated phrase
to find some meaning

so the lesson was abstracted
pregnant with pertinence and prehension

i was looking for a repeated phrase
till it issued its spark

Turned Over by Her Own Allies

in the prototype of a criminal trial
the poem is brought to earth,
brought to dictum, and put on the
Index

i call you to spectate in order to
be outfit for close contest

public enemy number one:
i have made it illiberal
the praise of fools has been
puffed up out of metaphor
to its real mechanics

the indictment: put to rout by
the sinew of the accusatrix
the cleverness and steady hand of
the annalist
will not unlock you this time
it only marks out the specific
crimes commissioned by
vocabulary

sentenced:
the juridic stands by, a bewitched
groundling, participating in the
looting of the mind
then assisting at the roadblocks
on the escape routes
from the shifting scene
acridly arresting the fugitives
and consigning them to the
raider as retinue

Dark Matter

half of the universe
is half of what
is not us

the artist has
a paint that
is not paint

we cannot do
without it
can not

The Mathematical Element

Calliope, Cassandra, the agelong
tellurian race against time, has
exhumed the natural selection,
and named a galaxy for Uriah Heep

so it makes headway, we pick
Dickens and not
the fanatical aborigine

stick together the atlas
stick at nothing
canter, canter,
and build your stately rhyme

the earthborn, cliff-dweller might
just eat the bread of radiation and
make virtue of our velocity

A Dirge for the Morning

he covered his head with black cistern
much of the water supply of the cities
was gathered there in the rainy season

he cracked the pit as a sign of mourning,
earth, land, panted for air like jackals
they snuffed up the wind like dragons

he was a wayfaring man, foreigner and
tourist with little concern for the drought
that touched the farmers, even wild animals

The Path I Took

when i was young
i thought all poets looked
like Robert Frost
with bushy eyebrows
and cardigan sweaters

but i sit here staring at a screen
in tee shirt
wiping my glasses with toilet paper
and no hope of
comparative relation

i can't scribble
with ink-covered fingertips
or walk in the woods with
dogs at my heels
and mental labor to be about

only this commission to
cut loose the leash
of lies that contrive
to throw off the scent
and words to pattern my good measure

Something Else

of stones and trees
we see
a way of speaking

when you say nature
it is in
a certain way

above and beyond
the actual facts
something else

we did not invent
but know
is to be obeyed

A Cadillac in Every Drive

i was baptized in a hot-tub,
pastor in fishing gaiters
beneath the white robe.

chlorine went up my nose as
i took the dunk for some
vague belief in a buyer's market.

i might even get good marks
by deserving them, being so
eclectic to his initiation.

so if i could put god into my
debt, he would handle his side
and put a cadillac in my drive.

i might even get a job that puts
me into the slow traffic of
the early risers. clock people.

in mere justice, my failures are
left to the chemicals, and the
prayers of the acceptable.

and the people who know me
say, forget the deals, and thank
the Lord, thank the Lord!

Our Suburban Landscape

suburbia is situated
on a volcano
passing through a fated
moment of languor

addressed to the very
conceptual soil, said to
surround the thickset
margin, bookends
of warm and cold
spings

to be called
the zone of
itinerancy,
natural channels
that surround
the central cone

Chokepoint

the narrow approach
looks so hard
to squeeze through
hands before head
then the heave
scraping shoulders
till you are
moored
with the effort
unable now to
knock or plead

There Can Be Little Excuse

my gross body has submitted nine days
that we should so long waive the wanting
of work to go unsaid and unpublished

the antiphonal chanting is the canary
at hand which i am about to use
it will be even more unheard of than
the abjurement has been

the words are pitched in the plural
since i am not leaving word to you alone
no doubt that the inhibition of calling you
into my meeting house will be just as
unheralded as the language set in print

For Three Sins...

shall we start with the distant
and each time the phrase is repeated
the circles are smaller
closer to home

to see if our sins differ
from the heathen

i can see it on a map
a topographic ocean
importing its waves
back to their spring

where ancestors never
lived or left

Political Developments

my silent years
are a secret name

matter and space
always have existed

a sort of fluke
of self-containment

to enjoy the us
of sectionalism

or more like a mind
than we know

like itself
of having minds

A Heavier Penalty

let patinaed accents dulcify
the feculence of wrath

so the pig will
splay runty

his independence squandered
on quarrels

where there is
no counterstatement

and vengence shall be
the golden ring in his snout

Advice for *Ulysses*

to calm passion
or lull the mindset
we will initiate another
kind of chaos
which will snub and slight
the understanding man

the novice will sit
in his seat
as presiding officer
of idiocracy

prefer me
before my peers
and i will tell you how
to make yourself
stinking rich
as if by
laughable happenstance

act the upstart and
speak as a bigot
                but,
like all artless actors
look inflated
and temporize
the name of insolance
and pride

The Currency of 30 Minutes

we are the nobodies
without the photomontage shakedown
or privilege proviso

neither Caesar nor celebrity
who move with the imposture of
parasitical insinuation

we are the commonwealth
of the obscure and neglected
to snap one's fingers at

by the indiscretion of cognizance
we will watch them climb
and labor to endow the occasion

To My Detractors

as i sustained my ordinary clay
for solemn initiative
you burst forth into assassination
by the act of laughter and
made game of its convictional sobriety

only by my ironbound hands
could the colonialism be marked-off

then i told them of the solemn promise
that had been put into words for me,
and what a climax this must have been
to your gales of risibility, the effect being
single-minded and already in sight

the charge sheet has already had
its price-cutting!

The Long Line

faithful to a steady
meter…
ca-clump, ca-clump,
of leaking tire,
leans me ever so
slightly towards
a lower shoulder.
but i will not
alter the tempo,
for highways are
napping and
lullabies
should have
consideration.

Watching the Wagon Roll

the wagon
seems
to be
going
nowhere, but
i
know that
it
is rolling.

Counting

it's only time
that
seems like such
a long rain
falling in
sheets all over
my patience.

i could be
lulled into
a mock exemption
from feeling
apologetic for
leaks in
the rafter.

The Hinge

entering doors
that do not
bay with a
conspicuous creak,
announcing
the manifest of
fleeting-figures,
is a haunting
premise.

some bathe hinges
in desirable oil,
where commodities
of the candid
are muffled
half-truths, while
some reveal the
gospel of
metallic frequencies.

Down on His Luck

everybody knows
he must
be insane

talking to
imponderable
angels

and nobody
hears
a thing

only the muffled
rain pouring
down in the night

an evil rain
eroding
suspicious spheres

Two Worlds

there is a membrane on the
water where some little bug,
with untold appendages,
skims along, leaving a
dwarfish imprint. a scar.
as two lurking eyes
beneath,
observe with fiendish
intent.

Perspective

the
wildflower
must
remind us
of all
that
is truly
relevant
just as
bees
must
bumble.

The Tempest

have you ever been told
it is nonsense to fear that which
cannot be avoided?

we, who faint and fear,
render up to this mania,

ask after ourselves
for what mainspring we are
so much disquieted,

on what ground,
what occasion,

to be pacified by reason,
contorted by some other object,
to a contrary passion.

Everlasting

from garage door to laundry room
you are!

before i ever spit up your endowment
there was a suitable quantum

and will be, continuous as the pirouetting
of my cottons and colors

and the cradle of dayspring
will grow weary-laden by midnight

Line of Work

when delicacy is consigned to
the lacking give of hardwood
all man-hour is without income

as in other orbits, the
bulging purse is excavated
along with the bare-handed
carrion

there is no antithesis
between the bilingual
text of poverty and the
worthy houses

the wages will turn to
nothing in the face of
life and death
the earnings soon to
be eroded

spare no nerve and sinew
to put in pawn blind bargains
when the need
of the hour is to
consider your atmosphere

The Palsy of Unbroken Sleep

to sleep upon that lower sleep
is the white radiance of reason
in the tenure of the treacherous

our etymology will denominate
our word-perfect
and closed-door narcotic chill

we will gauge the overgrowth
of satisfaction, sweet quietude,
and diplomacy of acute habit

this is not made plain with a
climate of opinion but the
aspiration of an acknowledgment

the pagan is entirely without
certification. nothing in his dialect
betrays any element of natural

language. simply one cannot
unriddle this earful, indeed we
end on a note of leeriness

Set Your Clock

when i am without daytime or nighttime
i will be known

when i have one name
the valley will be known

as the mountains move to the north
half will move south

at my second birth
my name will be a song

and the saints will
give voice

Prophesy and Delineation

the genius is the
living incarnation
of this marly stock

the unrevealed charge
to which all foreign
design is traced

manic libretto in
its higher
and lower forms

all will luxuriate
in dreams of
a faint suggestion

mediator of divine
revelation and
extraordinary universalism

To Cry for the Moon

so jesus said to be like doves
and you squatted to drop an egg
legs unstable, not sure from which
orifice it would leap out

developing perseverance, i saw
this on your two minds attempting
to evoke the inexpressible
symbols (harps, crowns, and gold)

The Reprobates of Agenda

the shopkeepers of this industry
will impregnate for a charge and
tell fortunes for felicity

the curfew will bring you
a nighttide without possession and
will obscure all your faces

you shall not have jurisdiction
as they recruit for atrocity and
call to the colors

but will not half of the eye
reproach itself and
libel all rational powers

Adding Up the Miles

it didn't matter anyway
that the houses weren't holy
and the faces looked so haunted.

because i'm in my car and
the radio's blasting away
to life's rich pageant.

still young despite the years,
the odometer is spinning
round to a new cadence.

it didn't matter anyway
that i was singing along with
such spirit and grace.

Porch Swing

we'll swing away
to another
world, you and i,
with legs
out before us,
smiling
side by side.

Lessons Lost

it taught me something, like
a good cigar with strong bite
and swirling intoxication does
when pulled away from puckered
       lips.
but my attention span is not the
same as earlier, so it was
forgotten, only to be replaced by
the story on the radio, about cheating love
       and all the times she
       left him.
so i was ready to go find that
cad, except i remembered that
the car is making noises, so
that thought had to be put on
       hold.
until the phone rang just once,
       yes just once.
now who could that have been,
to interrupt my rage? maybe
a shy admirer, or the idiot
with numbers, the one whose fingers
       are not connected
       to the brain.
but anyway, the cigar is becoming
a burning nub and my tongue is
caked with a film.

which brings me back to…
which brings me back to…
oh, hell,
i know there was a point to all this.

Signals

one pretty street
with arched
tree branches,
posing as
an elfin tunnel,
had a traffic
light spanning
the entrance.

red — the stop kind.

it narrowed to
an eclipse of
my reality.
and i began to
feel like
alice, so
big and
inquisitive, when
the light changed.

green — the drink me kind.

Split-second

the image of
what
for one second
seemed
completely peculiar
was
only a
reminder that
the
awkward
can be remarkable

Americas

a home for visions
of...
spanish guitars serenading
lovers on any street
corner, locked as one and becoming
the music.

sisters who balk at
poverty,
splashing and snickering
in the soft current
of at least one tributary.
[me encantaria]

the virgin mother
whose
skin is brown
and
words are mestiza;
with raw
significance.

a new vocabulary.

The Dilemma of Desire

this is a body of water,
encased by things
other than itself.
it is the one we love most,
when the intervention of
light can reflect
our coagulation.
and we can look upon this
image without the need or
deficiency to satiate
our sins.
it is only a need to
drink from it that quenches
that proclivity.

Where My Brother Builds Castles

this place is now at your command
the sand is cool and pliable
and castles are your fortress
to expel the onslaught
welsh archers at your disposal
entire cities to be chiseled
by the strength of your vision

this place is now at your command
a benevolent kingdom on the shore
where you had designed worlds for
the pleasure of clan and attendants
and we shall forever tread lightly
over this landscape of remembrance
for here sits a city on high

Among Orchids

she is a light
contiguous
virgin-white, tropical
breath—
amid heartened,
morning-shower orchids.

she is a delicious
tepid
sensual-expectation, delicately
flowering—
the measure
of desire, evolving.

Duet

poplars shimmered along the trail
where trappers sang to the sky.

coffee brewed on the campfires
and kindled the mountain spirits.

wind songs came swirling down
dancing from limb to limb.

river's bend, availed an oasis
where trappers sang to the sky.

Paradise Possible

maybe somewhere
there is a
place for all this love

before heaven claims
a world
with no more time

and rivers
abandon their steady
pulse

Night Woods

the path between the houses is dark.
twigs snap underfoot

hoping to avoid toads
with insect-filled bellies.

even blackness has shadows in this
haven of childhood fears,

a lair of beastly dominion, starting
heart to echo in breathless lungs.

the light ahead beckons as crickets
goad my quickened steps.

Dandelion Steam

there is a playground
worth conjuring
for the weathered
and weary

of hot blacktop and
uncomely
steel stretched into
blinding orbits

a zeal brought out to
soften the tar while
kick-stands slowly sink
and balance is lost

a field afar
lit up with yellow
dandelion steam
waits for the day

the glorious moment
when the boys of baseball
rally to the call
green with anticipation

Tip of the Tongue

i am looking for that word.
you know the one i mean.
letters connecting as empirical
testament to firing synapses.
tangible construction of concept.

if only chemistry were visual
and the world a projection screen,
you could remind me.
why it's not here only implicates
the mystery.

the oils on canvas are blending.
the primer is slowly fading under
a new brilliance, a harmony.
and the soft illusion ahead teeters
on the precipice of extinction.

About the Author

Mark Van Aken Williams grew up in Shaker Heights, Ohio and received a Master of Education and a Bachelor of Arts from Cleveland State University. Throughout his life, he's enjoyed traveling: including salmon fishing in Alaska, visiting Mayan ruins in the Yucatan Peninsula, deep sea fishing in Costa Rica and attending an International Rainforest Workshop on the Amazon River in Peru. He has been writing poetry and essays for many years and his work reflects a sensibility that extends beyond national borders and encompasses the dichotomy of poverty/wealth, striving/acceptance, ancient/modern, and the particular and universal.

When not traveling or writing, Williams enjoys cooking for friends and family and following soccer. He and his wife, Janice, live with three dogs and a parrot in the beautiful hills of Southeastern Ohio.

—❋—

www.markvawilliams.com
www.luckypress.com

2944756

Made in the USA